"Lucinda's Sprites" by T. DiTerlizzi

THE SPIDERWICK CHRONICLES

NOTEBOOK for FANTASTICAL OBSERVATIONS

T. DiTERLIZZI and H. BLACK

Simon and Schuster Books for Young Readers
New York   London   Toronto   Sydney

This notebook belongs to

SIMON & SCHUSTER BOOKS FOR YOUNG READERS
An imprint of Simon & Schuster Children's Publishing Division
1230 Avenue of the Americas, New York, New York 10020
This book is a work of fiction. Any references to historical
events, real people, or real locales are used fictitiously. Other
names, characters, places, and incidents are products of the
author's imagination, and any resemblance to actual events or
locales or persons, living or dead, is entirely coincidental.
Copyright © 2005 by Tony DiTerlizzi and Holly Black
All rights reserved, including the right of reproduction
in whole or in part in any form.
SIMON & SCHUSTER BOOKS FOR YOUNG READERS
is a trademark of Simon & Schuster, Inc.
Book design by Michael Nelson
The text for this book is set in Rackham Italic.
The illustrations for this book are rendered in pen and ink.
Manufactured in the United States of America
2 4 6 8 10 9 7 5 3 1
CIP data for this book is available
from the Library of Congress.
ISBN-13: 978-1-4169-0345-1 (hardcover)
ISBN-10: 1-4169-0345-3 (hardcover)
ISBN-13: 978-1-4169-5014-1 (paperback)
ISBN-10: 1-4169-5014-1 (paperback)

Additional thanks to Michael Nelson
for his extraordinary assistance in developing
the *Notebook for Fantastical Observations'* activities.

For all
writers, artists,
and readers
— Tony and Holly

Tony DiTerlizzi is the illustrator of the Caldecott Honor–winning *The Spider and the Fly* as well as the author and illustrator of the Zena Sutherland Award–winning *Ted*. He and his wife, Angela, reside with their pug, Goblin, in Amherst, Massachusetts. Visit Tony on the World Wide Web at www.diterlizzi.com.

～∞～

Holly Black is the author of *Tithe: A Modern Faerie Tale*, which the American Library Association selected as a YALSA Best Book for Young Adults as well as for the YALSA Teens' Top Ten Booklist. Holly lives in Amherst, Massachusetts, with her husband, Theo. Visit Holly on the Web at www.blackholly.com.

NOTE FROM THE AUTHORS

Dear Readers,

When Tony and I first heard the story of the Grace children, we thought that their experiences were unusual. Since then, however, children and adults alike have contacted us with their encounters with faerie. A few of them are presented in this book along with some exercises that we hope will help you investigate potential faerie activity where you live.

Above all, please remember to be careful. While some faeries are helpful, many are tricksy, and others can be dangerous.

Sincerely,

Holly Black

and

Tony DiTerlizzi

Map of
MY
NEIGHBORHOOD
and
Surrounding Areas

BROWNIE

"To protect the house and those inside
is MY duty, Guide or no Guide."

FROM BOOK 5: THE WRATH OF MULCARATH

BROWNIES

I admit I'm a slob. I throw my socks and underwear on the floor. I kick the covers off my bed and sleep on the bare mattress. My hair sticks up from my head like a bunch of crabgrass. I never clean up any of my toys. If something gets broken because I stepped on it, then I just try to avoid that area. Sometimes I forget, but usually there are enough clothes on top that the broken toy parts don't hurt my feet that bad. But no matter how messy I am, there is always someone messier than me.

My parents don't understand how I got to be this way. My room used to be neat, my hair combed and my clothes folded. That was when Skifflewhim was my friend. He's really little, with big hairy ears and pants made from an old leather glove. He would hop around, making my clothes dance themselves into the drawers. My hair would part and braid itself out before I even woke up, so I wouldn't notice if he worked on the tangles. My dolls would march right onto the shelves.

And all I had to do was leave out some scraps from dinner.

Skifflewhim liked everything I didn't. He would eat my brussels sprouts, my beets, and the liver my mom would fry with onions. I guess it was because he ate all that stuff that I started to wonder what he wouldn't eat. I left out a raw onion and he ate it. I left out a bunch of worms I dug up out of the yard and he ate those too. Finally, I thought of the most disgusting thing I could: kitty litter.

When I came back from school, my

bed was unmade and the litter was thrown all over my room. Some of it was even in my sheets. Since then, I haven't seen Skifflewhim once, even when I left out a drumstick with only one bite taken out of it. But although I don't see him, I know he's there. Books sometimes just fall off the shelves. Lightbulbs burn out extra fast. My clothes are ripped and my homework goes missing.

So, you see, I have to be as messy as possible. That way he can't make it any worse. Until I figure out a better idea, that's what I'm going to do.

—Kelly L.

ANALYSIS: Brownies are known to be helpful, but if angered they can turn into troublesome boggarts. This appears to be a case of such a transformation.—H. B. & T. D.

I imagine this creature helping me with chores around my house:

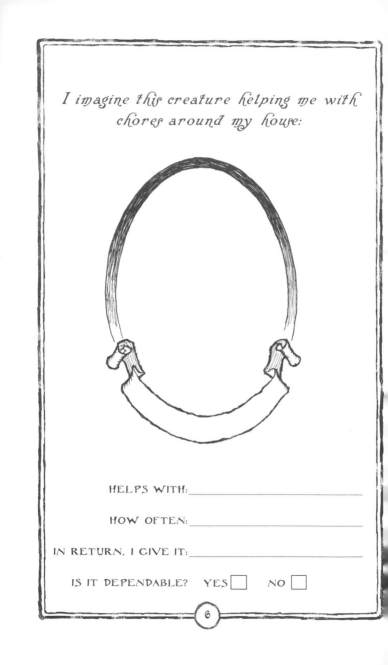

HELPS WITH:_____

HOW OFTEN:_____

IN RETURN, I GIVE IT:_____

IS IT DEPENDABLE? YES ☐   NO ☐

Here's what else I know about it:

_____

_____

_____

_____

_____

_____

_____

_____

_____

_____

_____

_____

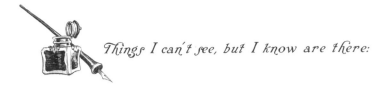

Things I can't see, but I know are there:

1. _____
2. _____
3. _____
4. _____
5. _____
6. _____
7. _____
8. _____
9. _____
10. _____
11. _____
12. _____
13. _____

Things I see, but I know aren't there:

1. _____

2. _____

3. _____

4. _____

5. _____

6. _____

7. _____

8. _____

9. _____

10. _____

11. _____

12. _____

13. _____

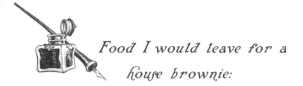

Food I would leave for a house brownie:

1.
2.
3.
4.
5.
6.
7.
8.
9.
10.
11.
12.
13.

Food I would not leave for a brownie:

1. _____
2. _____
3. _____
4. _____
5. _____
6. _____
7. _____
8. _____
9. _____
10. _____
11. _____
12. _____
13. _____

A drawing of my room when it's a mess:

A drawing of my room after being cleaned by a brownie.

A floor plan of my house showing locations of possible brownie activity:

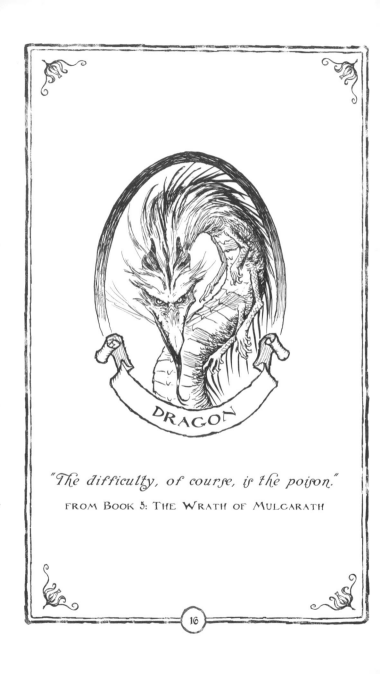

DRAGON

"The difficulty, of course, is the poison."

FROM BOOK 5: THE WRATH OF MULGARATH

DRAGONS

Sometimes my brother, Ross, and I hunt for bugs in the old woodpile behind the house. You can find huge black beetles, little pill bugs that curl up into pale gray balls, earwigs with scary pincers, and occasionally blind and twisting worms that you can cut in half to make two short ones.

We like to make the bugs fight inside a cup, but they won't always attack one another, even if you shake them around. Once we took a bucket and gave two click beetles and a worm a place to live, but the next day the click beetles were gone and the worm was dead. Mostly, the fun part is finding and catching the bugs.

I always hoped that we would find something way cool, like a frog or a mouse, and one day we did find something—a lizard. It was black, but when it moved, colors shifted along its back the way they do along the surface of oil. My brother slammed both hands over it fast, picked it up, and started running toward the house. Halfway there, he yelled like he got stung by a bee and dropped the little lizard in the grass. I figured it must have bit him, so I looked around for anything I could put between my hands and it. There was an old bucket, half-filled with rainwater, not too far off. Dumping out the water and splashing my sneakers in the process, I ran over to where the lizard was. The black body slithered through the grass as I dropped the bucket over it.

Ross held up his hand. Tiny tooth marks indented the pinkish skin. It didn't look that bad, but his eyes were all watery and I thought he was going to cry.

"Get something to slide under the bucket," I said to distract him.

He went into the house and came back a few minutes later with flattened cardboard. We pushed it under the bucket fast and then flipped the whole thing over. I scanned the grass in case it got away and Ross kicked the sides of the bucket to knock it off the ceiling or the walls. Then we pulled off the top.

The little black lizard was in there, looking small and harmless against all that white plastic.

"Cool," I said.

We brought the bucket inside and I watched the lizard while my brother cleaned out an old fish tank from the basement. He filled the bottom with dirt from outside and taped the lighted top on tight enough so that the lizard couldn't get out through any of the openings. We dumped the lizard in the tank and watched it for a couple of minutes. Then Mom called us

to do some chore and I didn't think about
the lizard again until that night, when Ross
complained that his arm hurt.

I was already in bed, so I turned over
and looked at him. His arm was hidden in
the sleeve of his pajamas. "Does it hurt
real bad?" I asked.

"Yeah," he said, his voice thinning to a
whine.

"Where does it hurt?" I asked.

"All over," he said.

I was unimpressed with that answer.
I mean, come on. Shouldn't he at least
know where it hurts? That was the kind
of answer I gave when I wanted to
stay home from school, but wasn't sick.
I yawned. "See if it feels better in the
morning," I said, then turned over and
went to sleep.

I woke up to see my mother sitting on
Ross's mattress. She had him out of his

pajama top and I could see thin threads of red and black running up and down his arm. The forearm and hand looked small and wrinkled—shrunken. He was crying and I felt bad and also, pretty scared. I didn't say anything to him and he didn't tell Mom about what I'd said the night before.

After she left to take him to the hospital, I took the fish tank outside, dumped out the lizard, and stomped on it until it was mush.

—Gavin G.

ANALYSIS: Even when a dragon is small, its poison can be very potent. The efficacy of the poison increases with the size of the dragon, so it was best the creature was encountered when still small.   —H. B. & T. D.

If I caught this creature:

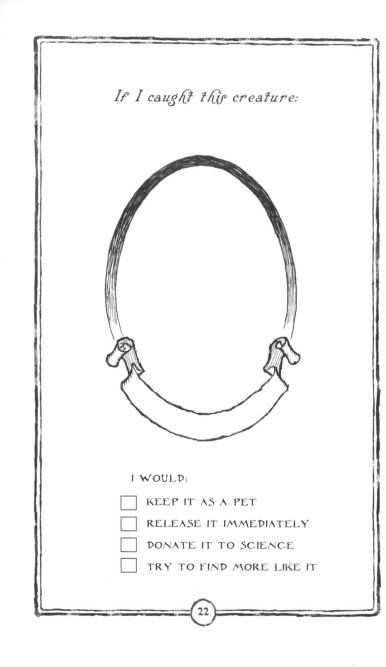

I WOULD:

- ☐ KEEP IT AS A PET
- ☐ RELEASE IT IMMEDIATELY
- ☐ DONATE IT TO SCIENCE
- ☐ TRY TO FIND MORE LIKE IT

Here's what else I know about it:

_____

_____

_____

_____

_____

_____

_____

_____

_____

_____

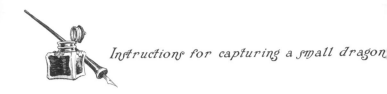

Instructions for capturing a small dragon

1. {see figure A}

{figure A}

2. {see figure B}

{figure B}

{figure C}

3.
{see figure C}

4.
{see figure D}

{figure D}

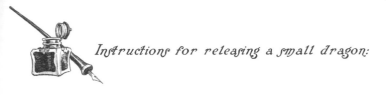

Instructions for releasing a small dragon:

1. _____

{see figure A}

_____

_____

_____

_____

{figure A}

2. _____

{see figure B}

_____

_____

_____

_____

{figure B}

{figure C}

3

{see figure C}

_____

_____

_____

_____

_____

{figure D}

4

{see figure D}

_____

_____

_____

_____

_____

A diagram of the terrarium in which I would keep a pet dragon:

Sketches of two locations where dragons may be found:

1. *in the real world:*

in the faerie world:

DWARF

"We will rebuild the world
in silver and copper and iron."

FROM BOOK 4: THE IRONWOOD TREE

DWARVES

I have this ball from when I was a kid. It's made from pure gold that shines like the sun. If you put your fingers just right on the surface and turn it—just so—the ball will open up. Inside is a jump rope of silver filigree as fine as a skein of thread, and an eight-sided die with drawings on each side for a game I only half-remembered. People ask me if it's real. They ask me where I got it, too, but I never tell them.

I used to have this friend who went by the name of Soltieg. I never saw him at school, but sometimes I'd see him around the neighborhood and then we would play games that none of the other kids knew. He was short, with black hair that stuck up from his head at odd angles and that he would tug at when he was nervous.

Sometimes he would come over to my house. We would microwave pizza bagels and watch television. He really loved cartoons and we'd spend hours watching the tube or playing with action figures in front of it. But after a while I wanted to go to his house. At first he made excuses.

"My house is too far away," Soltieg said.

"Then why are you always around here?" I asked him.

He pulled on his hair. "We don't have a television."

I shrugged.

He sighed. "My parents wouldn't like it."

"Fine," I said, but the way I said it, he could tell that it wasn't fine.

A week later he gave in and told me he was going to take me to his place. We cut through my neighbor's backyard and the woods behind their house. We lived beside some steep hills, but as the road snaked upward, Soltieg led me up to the edge of the rocks where there were no houses.

"Where are we going?" I asked.

He pointed to a shadowed area and an entrance to what looked like a cave. I forgot all about going to his place. A cave! That was about the coolest thing I could imagine. It was damp and a little chilly inside, but I didn't mind. I thought of making a fort or a clubhouse with lots of rules about who got in. I was just thinking up what the first rule should be when I noticed that there were torches flickering in the gloom. They burned with a strange blue fire.

"This is where I live," Soltieg said. "I'll take you all the way in if you promise not to tell anyone about it and promise that you won't try and bring anything from inside of the cave back out."

"Sure," I said. "No problem."

He led me into a vast cavern. There was a whole city inside, made from gleaming gold and shining silver. Gems as large as grapes ornamented spires and hung from bronze trees as though they really were fruit. Overhead, even the distant ceiling of the cave had been painted with gold and hung with opals that mimicked stars. Occasionally a mechanical butterfly would fly by, its wings rising and falling in time with the key unwinding at its side. As I walked through the streets cobbled with marble, I noticed that all the inhabitants of this strange city were shorter than I was—even the ones with beards.

Soltieg brought me to his home, which was a modest house on a sloping street, but still crafted from stone so polished that it reflected like a mirror. The whole place was topped off with a roof of glinting copper. He took me inside and we played a dice game with rubies, a board game where the pieces were warriors blown from glass, and a card game with cards that were etched in gold.

His mother brought us dishes of things I couldn't identify dressed in unfamiliar spices and with many sauces. Despite not usually being a fan of weird food, I ate all of mine.

Before I knew it, it was time to go back. I didn't want to go. It didn't seem fair that Soltieg got to live in a magical place. Even though his mother told me I could come again tomorrow, I found myself overcome with anger and envy.

I slipped the golden ball into my pocket. It wasn't that I forgot about my promise; it was just that I figured the promise meant I better not get caught. I deserved it anyway—he had all of this; why should he miss one little toy? Following Soltieg to the entrance, the golden ball seemed hot in my sweaty grip, but to tell him now would get me in too much trouble. I said good-bye and Soltieg said good-bye back, but his voice was sad and one of his hands tugged at his hair.

After that, I never saw him again. When I went to try to find the cave, the stone was solid. There was no entrance into the mountain.

All I had was the golden ball.

—Eric N.

ANALYSIS: Dwarves are fine metalworkers with a deeply felt sense of honor.

—H. B. & T. D.

*An odd little creature I've seen
around my neighborhood:*

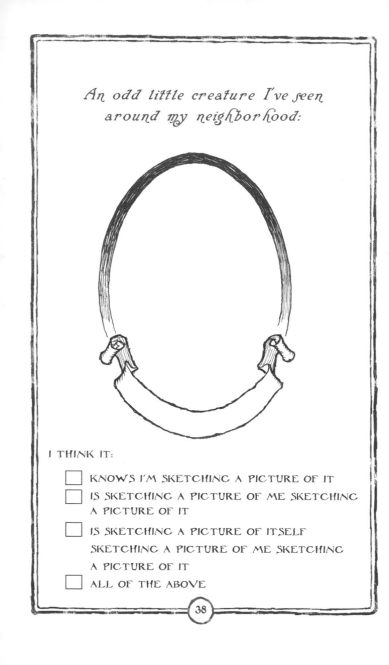

I THINK IT:

☐ KNOWS I'M SKETCHING A PICTURE OF IT

☐ IS SKETCHING A PICTURE OF ME SKETCHING
A PICTURE OF IT

☐ IS SKETCHING A PICTURE OF ITSELF
SKETCHING A PICTURE OF ME SKETCHING
A PICTURE OF IT

☐ ALL OF THE ABOVE

Here's what else I know about it:

_____

_____

_____

_____

_____

_____

_____

_____

_____

_____

_____

My three favorite

board games: **1.** _____

2. _____

3. _____

card games: **1.** _____

2. _____

3. _____

games that only me and my best friend know:

1. _____

2. _____

3. _____

Promises I've made:

_____

_____

_____

_____

_____

Promises I've broken:

_____

_____

_____

_____

_____

_____

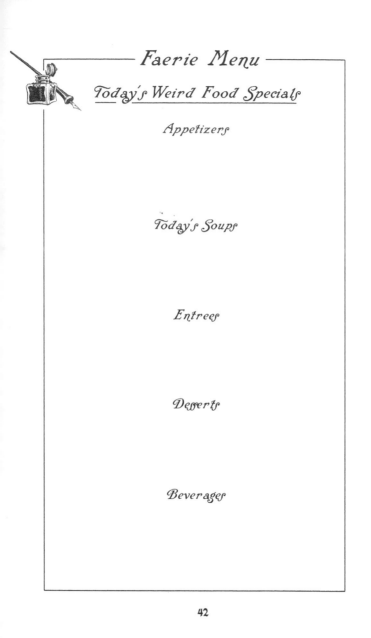

Faerie Menu

Today's Weird Food Specials

Appetizers

Today's Soups

Entrees

Desserts

Beverages

My Favorite Faerie Food Recipe

Ingredients

Tools

Preparation

Serving Suggestions

My drawing of the most magical place to live:

Sketches of exquisite metal jewelry handcrafted by dwarves:

1. Rings:

2. Earrings:

3. Amulets:

A picture of my left hand drawn with my right:

A picture of my right hand drawn with my left:

ELF

"We make our homes in the sparse forests left to us. Soon even those will be gone."

FROM BOOK 3: LUCINDA'S SECRET

ELVES

One night when Mandy and I were having a sleepover at her house, we got bored with watching videos on the little television on her dresser and with looking through fashion magazines.

"I'm hungry," I said.

She looked up. "There's nothing to eat here. You want to walk down to Quick Stop?"

It was very, very late and we knew that we weren't supposed to go out. Her parents were zonked out, though, her mom snoring gently, and we figured that no one would notice. We pulled on jackets and sweaters over our pajamas and tiptoed to the door.

Outside it was warm and a little damp from dew. I took a deep breath of summer air and fresh-mown lawns. Mandy did a little dance in the middle of the empty road. It was weird to be out there in the middle of the night—as if, while everyone else was sleeping, the world was ours and ours alone.

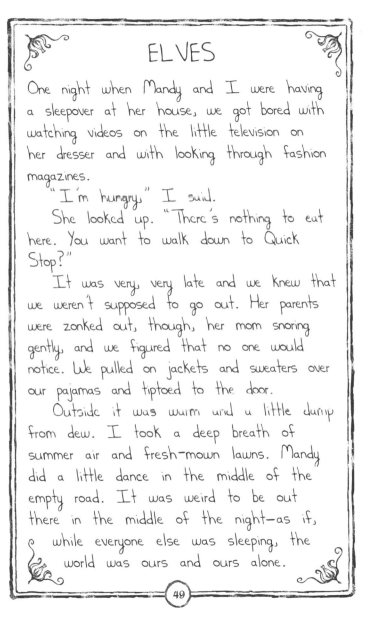

At the store we bought a package of doughnuts and two cans of soda and laughed at the way the clerk stared at our pajamas while we paid. Feasting as we walked back, we didn't notice the music at first.

It was almost discordant, almost noise, but there was something about the sounds that made them compelling. The notes were so pure, the melodies so beautiful, even as they crashed against one another.

Mandy grinned and wiped off the powder that dusted her lapel. "Maybe it's a band practicing."

"It's probably just someone with a CD." I pulled on her sleeve. "Let's go home." I didn't know what or who it was, but I didn't want to find out. I liked the feeling of being a little bad and sneaking out, but I wasn't sure I wanted to hang out with some weird people I didn't know. I just wanted to be with Mandy, drink soda, eat crappy food, and gossip.

Mandy barely noticed me. She was already walking toward the wooded area that the music came from. I had no choice but to follow her.

We walked for a while, the tall weeds soaking the hems of my pajama pants. The music swelled, but we still saw nothing.

The summer breeze rustled the leaves of the trees and with it, I thought I heard a voice. "Come dance," it called. "Come dance."

"I'm going back," I said, but all I did was go no further. Mandy walked on. After a while, the music faded and I figured she'd come back, but she didn't. I stood there and stood there. Finally I tried to follow the way she'd gone. I called her name, but she didn't answer. Despite all my looking that night, the search parties that came later, the newspaper articles, and the backs of milk cartons, no one ever saw Mandy again.

—Linda L.

ANALYSIS: Elves sometimes dance in faerie rings. It is said that if a human joins their dance, he or she can be spirited away for years and sometimes forever. Often, a loose circle of toadstools will be the only evidence of the faerie dancing.   —H. B. & T. D.

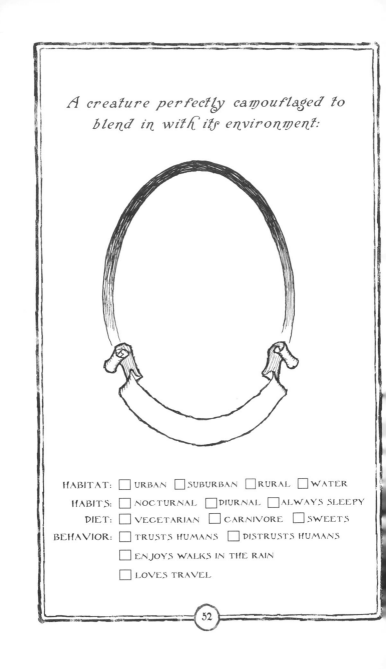

A creature perfectly camouflaged to blend in with its environment:

HABITAT: ☐ URBAN ☐ SUBURBAN ☐ RURAL ☐ WATER

HABITS: ☐ NOCTURNAL ☐ DIURNAL ☐ ALWAYS SLEEPY

DIET: ☐ VEGETARIAN ☐ CARNIVORE ☐ SWEETS

BEHAVIOR: ☐ TRUSTS HUMANS ☐ DISTRUSTS HUMANS

☐ ENJOYS WALKS IN THE RAIN

☐ LOVES TRAVEL

Here's what else I know about it:

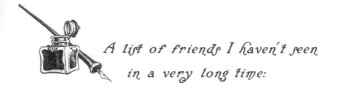

*A list of friends I haven't seen
in a very long time:*

A nighttime adventure I've had that
my parents don't know about:

_____

_____

_____

_____

_____

_____

_____

_____

_____

_____

_____

_____

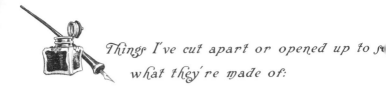

Things I've cut apart or opened up to see what they're made of:

1.

2.

3.

4.

5.

6.

7.

8.

9.

10.

11.

12.

13.

Things I can do to help protect the environment and make sure faeries always have a home:

1.

2.

3.

4.

5.

6.

7.

8.

9.

10.

11.

12.

13.

Leaf rubbings:

Pictures of the weirdest bugs
I've ever seen:

Pictures of bugs that give me the creeps:

GOBLIN

"Fidirol, Fidirat!
Catch a dog, catch a cat
Skin it raw, skin the fat
On the spit, turn like that
Fidirol, Fidirat!"

FROM BOOK 2: THE SEEING STONE

GOBLINS

When my dad got a new job teaching at a university, we had to move to a town nearby it. It wasn't that different from our old town, so my dad was surprised when the neighbors warned us about animals getting into our garbage cans. At the old house, sometimes squirrels would get into the trash if we put it out too early or something, but it wasn't anything we had to be warned about. Mom said our neighbor must think we were city people or something and didn't have any common sense.

That was until we found our new plastic garbage can with the handles still locked and a hole gnawed in the side.

"What could do that?" Mom asked.

"Maybe raccoons," I said.

"Raccoons my a—," said Dad.

Mom frowned at him.

"Sorry." He looked at me.

I grinned.

We bought new cans, metal ones this time, and a Havahart trap big enough to catch a bobcat. Mom baited it with some gnawed-on chicken drumsticks from dinner the night before and we left it out by the garage where the trash cans rested when they weren't sitting out at the curb.

Nothing much happened that night, but when I got home from school the next day, I checked the trap. Inside was the hugest, most disgusting frog I'd ever seen. Its blubbery body actually pressed against the hatched metal sides of the cage. It rocked back and forth—something I didn't think frogs could do—and when I walked closer, it turned its gold-flecked eyes in my direction.

"Hey," it said, voice rough and croaky. "Let me go."

"Mom!" I yelled, and ran for the house.

She was washing carrots in the sink when I found her. I pulled her outside. We both looked at the giant frog.

"It told me to let it go," I said, feeling, I admit, like a bit of a tattler.

She laughed. "It sure looks like it would say that, doesn't it? Let's just leave it alone until your father gets home. Maybe he'll know what to do with it."

With that, Mom went back inside. As

I turned back toward the cage, out of the corner of my eye I could have sworn I saw the frog smile and I could have sworn that it had a mouthful of sharp teeth.

"I know you can talk," I said.

"I can," said the frog. "Now let me out. The metal burns my skin. It is very ouchey."

"You bit a hole in our trash can," I said.

"No, no." It bugged out its eyes even more. It might have been trying to make an innocent face, but it wasn't doing a very good job. "Not me."

"Are there more of you?" I asked, looking around. "Did one of them do it?"

"Maybe," said the frog.

I squatted down by the cage. There really did appear to be scorch marks striping the creature's skin. "What ARE you?"

"What will you give me if I tell you?" it rasped.

"Nothing," I said.

It gurgled a little.

I got up and brushed off my jeans like I was going to walk away.

"Wait," it croaked. "Goblin."

"What?"

"I'm a goblin. Let me out and I'll give you something."

"Give me what?" I asked. I was thinking of magic wishes, but I was also concerned that I might have to kiss that enormous green lump. There wasn't much I wanted enough to put my lips on that. Then the first part of what it'd said filtered into my brain. "A goblin?"

"How about me and my friends don't bite your things. No eating cans or cats nothing."

"You eat cats?" I felt like all I was doing was repeating the last thing the goblin said.

"Kittens better," it said. "Not so chewy."

"I don't think I should let you out," I said.

"You like kittens? Okay, I'll promise not to eat any cats. Nothing from your house and no cats."

"Forever?" I asked.

It grunted and groaned, but finally it said, "Forever."

I opened the latch and let it shuffle out. For a moment the shape shimmered and I thought I saw another shape, something still froggy, but more upright and with claws. Then it jumped into a patch of thick weeds at the border of our neighbor's yard and disappeared from sight.

Dad was disappointed, of course, but I told him that frogs didn't have the teeth to bite through a garbage can and we couldn't hold it without more than circumstantial evidence. My dad said I needed to stop watching cop shows.

The goblin must have stuck to his side of the bargain because our trash was never troubled again, even when it was put out a day too soon or overripe with party trash. I saw lots more cats in the neighborhood and felt pretty good about that, at least until the day my neighbor's pair of long-haired pet rabbits disappeared.

—Devon L.

ANALYSIS: Goblins are malicious scavengers that can be dangerous in groups. Luckily, this one seems to have been willing to strike a bargain.
                                        —H. B. & T. D.

*This creature might
eat our trash:*

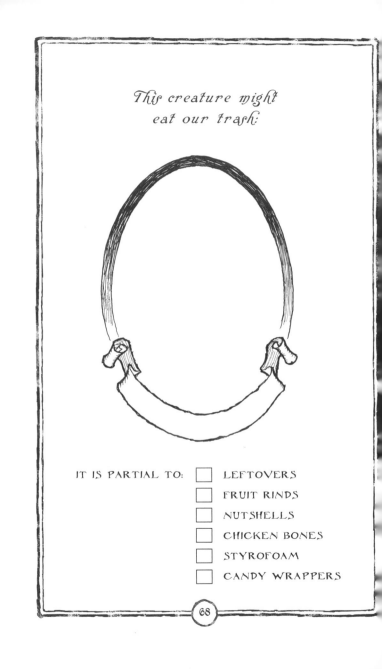

IT IS PARTIAL TO:

☐ LEFTOVERS

☐ FRUIT RINDS

☐ NUTSHELLS

☐ CHICKEN BONES

☐ STYROFOAM

☐ CANDY WRAPPERS

Here's what else I know about it:

_____

_____

_____

_____

_____

_____

_____

_____

_____

_____

_____

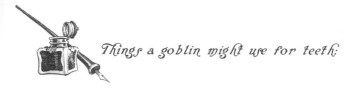

Things a goblin might use for teeth:

1. _____

2. _____

3. _____

4. _____

5. _____

6. _____

7. _____

8. _____

9. _____

10. _____

11. _____

12. _____

13. _____

Things I like about visiting the dentist:

1. _____

2. _____

3. _____

4. _____

5. _____

6. _____

7. _____

8. _____

9. _____

10. _____

11. _____

12. _____

13. _____

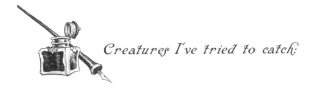

Creatures I've tried to catch:

1. _____

2. _____

3. _____

4. _____

5. _____

6. _____

Creatures I've caught:

1. _____

2. _____

3. _____

4. _____

5. _____

6. _____

Creatures I've caught accidentally:

1. _____

2. _____

3. _____

4. _____

5. _____

6. _____

Creatures I'm glad I haven't caught:

1. _____

2. _____

3. _____

4. _____

5. _____

6. _____

My drawing of the cutest house pet imaginable:

My drawing of the ugliest house pet imaginable:

"The Case of the Missing Kitty"
A Goblin Mystery

Not long ago . . .

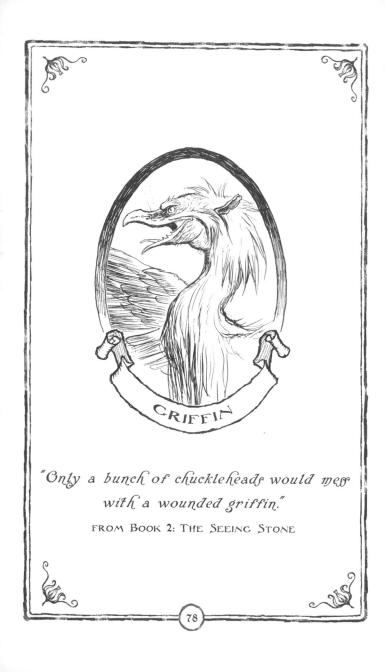

GRIFFIN

"Only a bunch of chuckleheads would mess
with a wounded griffin."

FROM BOOK 2: THE SEEING STONE

GRIFFIUS

When I was eleven, my older brother brought home two puppies. They were little white balls of curly fur with undershot teeth and tiny pink eyes. Some neighborhood dog had given birth and the owners were giving them away to any sucker that walked by. John hid the puppies up in his room, but Mom and Dad heard their little nails scratching over the wooden floors and busted him. They yelled and yelled, but he promised that he would walk them and feed them and train them. Finally, half-convinced, they looked over at me, lurking in the hallway, and asked what I thought. I told them that as long as the puppies weren't allowed in my room, I didn't care. I was afraid of dogs. I think my dad let John keep them mostly because I said that. My dad was big on confronting your fears.

John got bored with the dogs fast. He named them Voltron and Vexxor and liked to chase them around the yard, but the only thing he ever taught them was how to jump high enough to bite your fingers and scratch your pants. My parents yelled at him, but it was in that half-hearted, I-told-you-so-but-what-can-I-do? way that meant he wasn't really in that much trouble. It was around then that we figured out that Voltron was actually a girl. It turns out that she was going to have puppies of her own. Mom took both dogs over to get them "fixed" after the puppies were born, but by then, it was way too late.

We soon had eight new puppies, meaning we had ten dogs total. They ran in a pack, peed on the furniture, and chewed up anything that hit the floor. In desperation, my parents locked them out in the backyard during the day with a couple of dog igloos. They ruled the lawn, digging pits in the dirt and fighting with one another until their white fur was muddy gray. At night, we had to bring them in because they barked so much they would have kept the whole neighborhood awake. The dogs would run through the house, nipping at our fingers, fighting on top of our laps, and jumping onto the dining room table to eat any leftovers.

I locked myself in my room. It was

the only place I was safe.

Then, one day, one of the dogs—Wibbles—went missing. He was just gone. The fence was still there, secure as ever, and there was no sign of a disturbance. My mother seemed worried, but I think she was just pretending. My dad didn't bother.

"Hopefully it won't come back," Dad said.

John looked in all the holes and behind all the shrubs, but he couldn't find the dog. The next day, another one was gone. The rest of the dogs seemed subdued, too, like they were worried.

The next day another dog disappeared. Each day we lost another one. My brother's distress grew.

John accused our dad. "You're doing this," he said.

Dad just laughed. "Kiddo, if I was going to get rid of those dogs, I wouldn't bother doing it one at a time."

I sneezed, which was good because it covered my laugh. I was just getting a cold and was busy holding my mug of chicken soup above the reach of the remaining dogs.

My brother made a face and whispered

to me, "If Mom keeps you home tomorrow," he said, "can you try and figure out what's happening?"

"I guess," I said, thinking that if I didn't, he would never know.

But the next day, I found myself pretty curious. I was alone in the house—Mom had made me buttered toast and tea, then headed off to work—so I put on my robe and sat at the kitchen table and watched the dogs out the window. It would have been boring normally, but I was sick enough that that was about all I had the energy to do.

Late in the afternoon I saw a shadow darken the lawn. Then a huge creature swooped down out of the sky, grabbed a dog in its claws, and flew off. It was massive, with a body like a lion and a head, wings, and talons like an oversized hawk.

I ran to the door and stared up at the sky, but it was already far enough away that it just looked like an oddly shaped bird. But there, blowing on the lawn, was a single feather as long as my forearm. I picked it up, touching the soft barbs of the vane, admiring the pattern of browns that played over its surface.

I grabbed the last dog and brought it inside. Without the rest of the pack, it was pretty quiet. I felt bad enough to feed it half of my peanut butter sandwich. We kept the dog in the house for the next week and a half, even though my brother didn't believe my story and my mother thought I had been feverish. By the time they insisted we let the dog out again, the thing must have been gone. I keep looking up at the skies, though, just in case it ever comes back looking for something bigger than a dog to eat.

—William G.

ANALYSIS: Griffins roost in high places and fly over large areas, scouting for food. Often this food source is a herd of sheep or an overpopulation of deer, but in this case the food source was something entirely different.

—H. B. & T. D.

This friendly creature is a combination of two animals:

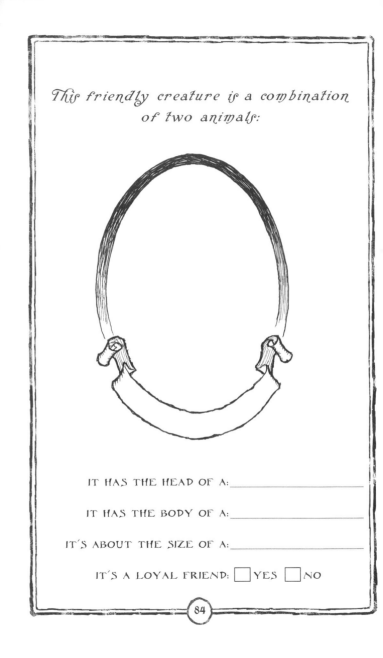

IT HAS THE HEAD OF A:_____

IT HAS THE BODY OF A:_____

IT'S ABOUT THE SIZE OF A:_____

IT'S A LOYAL FRIEND: ☐ YES ☐ NO

Here's what else I know about it:

Things I've seen that scare me:

1. _____

2. _____

3. _____

4. _____

5. _____

6. _____

7. _____

8. _____

9. _____

10. _____

11. _____

12. _____

13. _____

Things I can't see that scare me:

1. _____

2. _____

3. _____

4. _____

5. _____

6. _____

7. _____

8. _____

9. _____

10. _____

11. _____

12. _____

13. _____

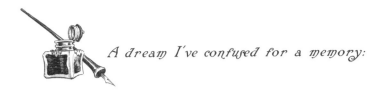

A dream I've confused for a memory:

Memories I have that may not actually be mine:

If I could be any animal or combination of animals for a day, I would look like this:

This is me in my favorite disguise:

A Griffin's-Eye
View of
MY
NEIGHBORHOOD

HOBGOBLIN

"Come on, Dumbellina, tell me you don't
believe in the tooth fairy!"

FROM BOOK 2: THE SEEING STONE

HOBGOBLINS

This thing moved in under my bed after my front tooth fell out. Now it shows up at night to pinch me. I know it's not the cat because the cat has a bell.

I've named him Puddingtoe because it sounds funny.

He also makes creepy shadows by wiggling his fingers in front of the night-light. I hope he stops really soon.

— Sam M.

ANALYSIS: More capricious than malicious, these pranksters can make a lot of trouble but are usually harmless. —H. B. & T. D.

This creature keeps me up at night:

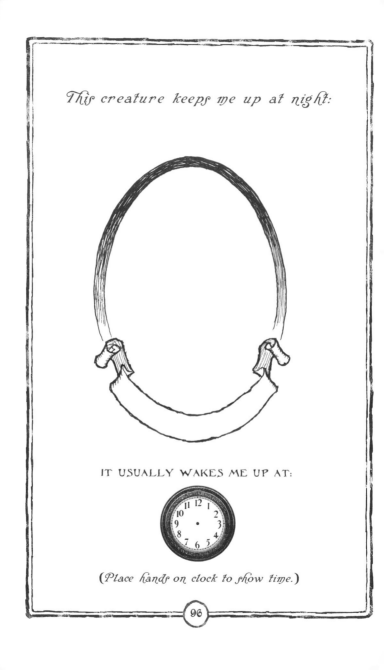

IT USUALLY WAKES ME UP AT:

(Place hands on clock to show time.)

Here's what else I know about it:

_____

_____

_____

_____

_____

_____

_____

_____

_____

_____

_____

I like to have a light on near my room at night because if I wake up I might:

_____

_____

_____

_____

_____

_____

_____

_____

_____

_____

_____

_____

When I wake during the night, familiar objects in my room appear to be these other things:

OBJECT:	WHAT IT APPEARS TO BE:
1.	
2.	
3.	
4.	
5.	
6.	
7.	
8.	
9.	
10.	
11.	
12.	

A list of funny names for creatures of the night:

	first syllable:	second syllable:	third syllable:
example:	Pud	ding	toe
1.			
2.			
3.			
4.			
5.			
6.			
7.			
8.			
9.			
10.			
11.			

full name:	full name with syllables in reverse order:
Puddingtoe	Toeingpudd

Some drawings of creepy shadows:

"Puddingtoe" drawing by Sam M.

Some more drawings of creepy shadows:

Postcard from a hobgoblin (front):

Greetings from

Postcard from a hobgoblin (back):

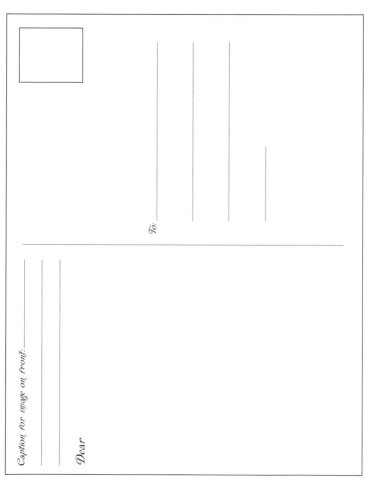

KNOCKER

"The stones. The stones speak.
They speak to me."

FROM BOOK 4: THE IRONWOOD TREE

KNOCKERS

TAP. TAP.

That is the sound I've been hearing every night in the new apartment. Since Dad lost his job, everything has been different. Before, we lived in a nice house. Now we have a cruddy apartment near where my two aunts live. My older sister, Maria, and I have to share a bedroom. A sheet divides the room, protecting Maria's "privacy." It doesn't protect me from Maria's snoring. And, of course, there's the other sound.

TAP. TAP.

I told Mom, but she said it was old pipes and I should ignore it. It gets in my head, though, cutting through my dreams, making it impossible to sleep. I'm tired all the time, stumbling through the halls of my new, scary school, but no one notices.

TAP. TAP.

Late one night I can't take it
anymore. The tapping seems to have started
earlier and is louder than usual. It bangs
around in my skull like loose dice. I get up
and stick my feet into my sneakers, not
even bothering to pop my heels in, letting
them squash the backs of the shoes. I
unlatch the front door, taking off the
chain and turning the bolt lock. Even
though Dad would have a fit, I wedge a
book in the door to keep it open and go
out into the hall.

TAP. TAP.

The hallway's worn blue carpet has
strings hanging off of it in places. The
other doors in the hallway look just like
ours. The sound is clearly coming from the
stairs, so I start down them. I hear a
television on at the second floor and a
dog barking on the first—even though we're

not allowed to have pets—but the sound is lower still. There's a numberless door to the basement and when I turn the knob, it opens.

TAP. TAP.

The stairs to the basement are rickety and it smells weird down here, like the stove does sometimes right before it lights. I swipe the dusty wall with my hand, looking for the light switch, but I don't find anything. The only light is a soft red glow from around the corner. I can feel my heart thumping away in my chest, in time with the steady tapping.

"Hello," I call, but my voice barely travels in the dark.

I take a step and the wood creaks under me. This is like a horror movie and I'm the really stupid heroine.

I get to the bottom and turn the corner. And there is a wrinkled little creature, all huge luminous eyes and skinny limbs. It's holding a pick-ax, which freaks me out because only serial killers seem to get a lot of use out of those, but after I look again I realize that the creature seems to be chopping a tunnel in the wall. It has stopped now, though, and it's staring at me and still holding the pick.

"You're keeping me awake," I say with mock bravado. "Can't you quiet down?"

"Noooo . . . must diiiig," it says in a voice that's little more than a whisper. "Gasssssss come from pipes. Slooooowly at first, like hissss of snake. Now worse. Choke or flame. Choke or flame. Must tunnel into a new building."

That's what the smell is. A gas leak.

I run up the three flights of stairs, run to our apartment, push open the door, and go right into my parent's room. I shake my dad's arm hard and he groans, eyelids fluttering.

"Gas leak," I say. My voice comes out somewhere between a shout and a squeak. It seems to work, though, because he nearly falls out of bed.

Together, we go down to the basement. The creature is gone, but the tunnel is still there. It seems like there might be light at the other end. Maybe the whatever-it-was actually made it into some other basement.

"You saved us, honey," Dad says.

But I didn't.

TAP. TAP.

—Keisha X.

ANALYSIS: At one time, knockers were found in mines and often warned miners of impending disasters. It is unclear what this one was doing in this apartment building.   —H. B. & T. D.

Here's a creature I would expect to find in most basements.

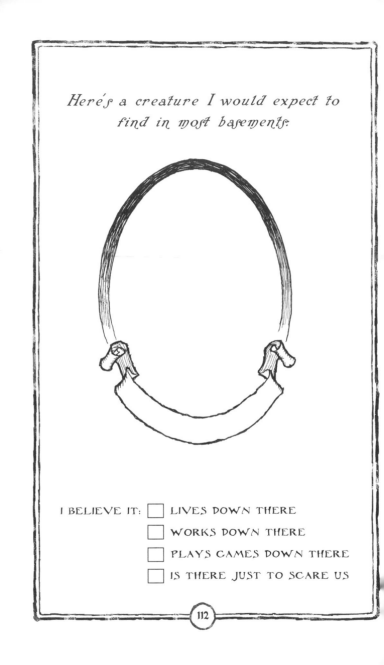

I BELIEVE IT:
- [ ] LIVES DOWN THERE
- [ ] WORKS DOWN THERE
- [ ] PLAYS GAMES DOWN THERE
- [ ] IS THERE JUST TO SCARE US

Here's what else I know about it:

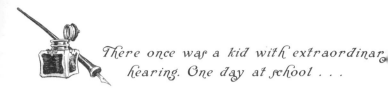

There once was a kid with extraordinary hearing. One day at school . . .

_____

_____

_____

_____

_____

_____

_____

_____

_____

_____

_____

_____

_____

An advertisement:

KNOCKER'S
Stone Listening
SERVICE

Let our experts help you:

_____

_____

_____

Our slogan:

_____

Free Estimates • Fully Insured
Residential or Commercial

Here's our money-back guarantee:

_____

_____

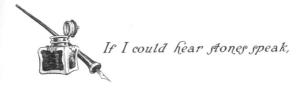

If I could hear stones speak,

1. *Mount Rushmore would tell me these facts:*

1. _____

2. _____

3. _____

4. _____

5. _____

6. _____

2. *Stonehenge would tell me these secrets:*

1. _____

2. _____

3. _____

4. _____

5. _____

The Rock of Gibraltar would tell me this fable:

My cover of a book about a creature that's able to hear the earth speak:

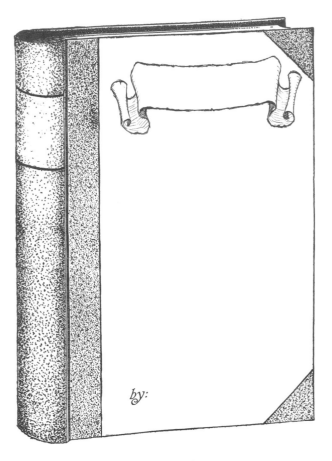

by:

My cover of a book about me:

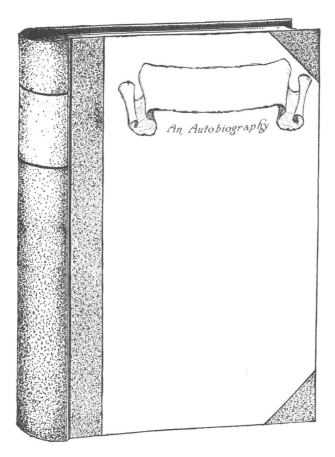

An Autobiography

Unusual objects I have found:

1. *Object:*

Description:

❷ *Object:*

detailed view:

Description:

OGRE

"They are master shape-shifters —
clever, sly, and cruel.
Strong, too, unfortunately."

FROM BOOK 5: WRATH OF MULCARATH

OGRES

I'm not a scaredy-cat or a yellow chicken or any of those other things people call me. You would have screamed too.

So, I was going for my Order of the Arrow badge. To get it, you have to wear a stick around your neck, not talk, and sleep out under the stars without a pillow or blanket or any kind of comfort. It's supposed to test your bravery.

But it's not like you're totally alone or anything. The scoutmaster puts up his tent and huddles in his cushy sleeping bag nearby. There's usually a bunch of us going for the Order at the same time, so even though it feels like you're alone outside, there's probably another kid not too far away from you.

So anyway, I brushed together a bunch of leaves and twigs and whatever. Then I kind of climbed into it, shoving the stuff over me so just my head was visible.

My plan was to combine camouflage and insulation. You know how if you get stuck out in the snow, you should build an igloo, because it is actually warmer? I thought that this would work the same way.

After I was settled, I had to try not to think about the weird scratchy feeling of all that stuff on top of me. It made me wonder what kind of worms or bugs could be crawling over my skin. I was concentrating so hard on that, I almost didn't see the bear.

I bet you think that that's when I screamed. Well, I didn't.

Actually, I held completely, totally still. I think that's why he didn't notice me. He was a big bear with dull, brownish fur and a nose that gleamed wetly in the moonlight. He stood up on his hind legs and sniffed the air. For a terrible moment, I thought he was going to smell me. He thudded back onto all four paws, however, and walked a few more paces. But then he did something surprising—he changed.

Horns sprouted from his brow, his body

thinned, and for a single moment, I thought I saw his eyes become slitted and gold like a cat's. Then its legs got much longer, the bear claws morphing into black hooves. In one more blink of my eyes, I was looking at a stag. I must have made some small sound, because the deer-thing turned its liquid eyes toward me.

That's when I screamed. You would have too. If I hadn't shrieked my head off, it wouldn't have run away and the scoutmaster wouldn't have checked on all of us. If it wasn't for me, the rest of the Order of the Arrow candidates could have been picked off, one by one. I think I should have gotten the biggest badge of all.

—Steven R.

ANALYSIS: Ogres are shape-changers, so it is sometimes difficult to tell when you have seen one. In this case, however, it was the shape-changing that gave the ogre away for what it was.

—H. B. & T. D.

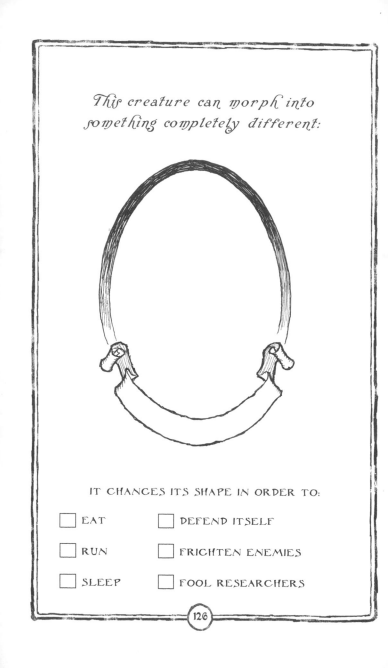

This creature can morph into something completely different:

IT CHANGES ITS SHAPE IN ORDER TO:

☐ EAT ☐ DEFEND ITSELF

☐ RUN ☐ FRIGHTEN ENEMIES

☐ SLEEP ☐ FOOL RESEARCHERS

Here's what else I know about it:

_____

_____

_____

_____

_____

_____

_____

_____

_____

_____

_____

True tefts of bravery:

 1.

 2.

3.

List of things I'd pack for a night in the woods:

1.

2.

3.

4.

5.

6.

7.

8.

9.

10.

11.

12.

13.

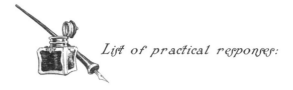

List of practical responses:

1. *What to do if you encounter a bear:*

1. _____

2. _____

3. _____

What NOT to do:

1. _____

2. _____

2. *What to do if you encounter an ogre:*

1. _____

2. _____

What NOT to do:

1. _____

2. _____

3 *What to do if you encounter a sprite:*

1. _____

2. _____

3. _____

What NOT to do:

1. _____

2. _____

4 *What to do if you encounter an extraterrestrial:*

1. _____

2. _____

3. _____

What NOT to do:

1. _____

2. _____

Creature trading cards:

1.

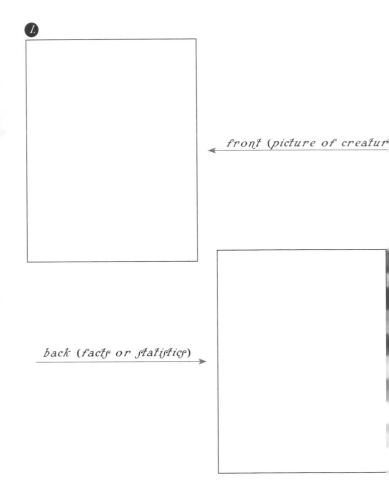

front (picture of creature

back (facts or statistics)

front (picture of creature)

back (facts or statistics)

Friend trading cards:

1.

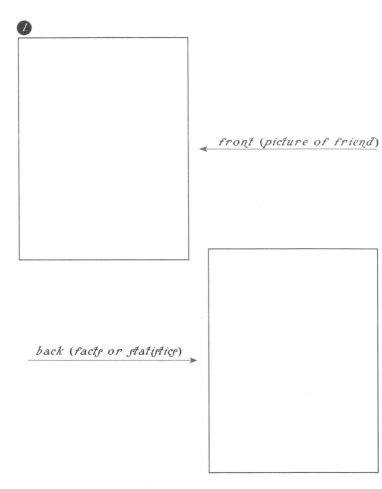

front (picture of friend) ←

back (facts or statistics) →

front (picture of friend)

back (facts or statistics)

PHOOKA

"The Black Dog of the Night. . . .
An afs or perhaps merely a sprite."

FROM BOOK 3: LUCINDA'S SECRET

PHOOKAS

I used to get beat up a lot at school. On the playground, I got hassled when the lunch monitors were looking the other way—but it wasn't too bad because no one wanted to get in too much trouble. The worst was actually before I even got to school and when I got home. A bunch of guys at my bus stop would push me and throw my backpack out into the street. One time they filled my mouth full of dirty snow and I tasted the grit all day long.

I think some people are born knowing the right things to wear and like to make themselves fit in (or be invisible). Not me. I have a loud, braying laugh, and when I'm nervous, I talk and talk and talk. But back then, no matter how cool I thought something was, no one else agreed with me. Like UFOs and aliens—I know tons about them, but whenever I said anything, the other kids would roll their eyes.

Things got so bad that I started pretending to be sick. I would look up diseases online and pretend to have them. The first day my stomach would hurt, the next day I would claim I saw purple spots in front of my eyes. At first my mother was worried and kept me home, but after a while she got skeptical. I had to resort to hiding in my room so she'd think I already left for school. The best spot was the hamper. No one ever looked in there. Eventually, though, she got wise to that, too, and—inevitably—I had to go to the bus stop again.

That morning I wound up in a

headlock with a bunch of kids giving me knuckle-burn noogies.

By the bus ride home, I was weighed down with books for make-up homework and dreading what might happen as soon as I stepped onto the sidewalk. One of the other kids, Marcus, squinted his eyes at me and then cracked his knuckles. I looked away.

At my stop, I got off the bus really slowly. I gathered up my stuff like a sleepwalker, hoping the other kids would just go home and leave me alone. They didn't, but something else was there too—a huge dog.

Its fur was a glossy black and its pink tongue lolled from between its teeth in a way that made it seem like the dog was smiling. As soon as Marcus stepped toward me, the dog growled.

"He yours?" one of the other kids—a guy named Kenny—asked.

I shook my head and took a step back. The dog seemed just as likely to bite me as to bite them. But when I started walking home, the dog walked at my side cheerfully. It walked right up to my door and then ran off.

The next day, when I started toward the bus stop, the dog was there again. It sat next to me while I waited for the bus and growled at anyone that bothered me. And so it went for weeks and weeks. The dog was my constant at the bus stop, guarding me from any harm. After a while, the other kids seemed to forget that they hated me and moved on to amusing themselves other ways.

One afternoon Kenny walked next to me and the dog on the way home. He told me about the book on spaceships he'd just read. I tried really hard not to correct his information.

"Does your dog have a name?" Kenny asked.

I petted the dog's soft fur and shook my head.

"You should name him."

"How about Shadow," I said, looking at the dog. "Would you like to be called Shadow?"

Shadow barked once. I didn't know if that was a yes or a no, but he walked me to my door just like he always did. The next morning, though, he wasn't waiting for me and I never saw him again.

—David T.

ANALYSIS: Phookas take the form of a black goat, rabbit, or dog. Although often tricksters, on some occasions phookas have been known to help people avoid danger.   —H. B. & T. D.

This creature is both scary
and cuddly:

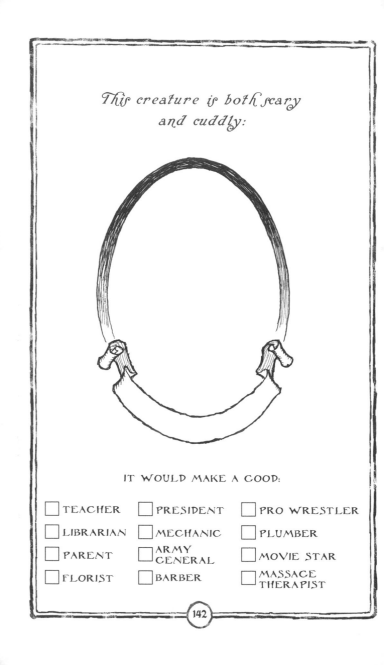

IT WOULD MAKE A GOOD:

☐ TEACHER   ☐ PRESIDENT   ☐ PRO WRESTLER

☐ LIBRARIAN   ☐ MECHANIC   ☐ PLUMBER

☐ PARENT   ☐ ARMY GENERAL   ☐ MOVIE STAR

☐ FLORIST   ☐ BARBER   ☐ MASSAGE THERAPIST

Here's what else I know about it:

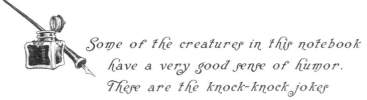

Some of the creatures in this notebook have a very good sense of humor. These are the knock-knock jokes I would share with them:

1.

Knock-knock.

Who's there?

answer: _____

question: _____ who?

punch line: _____

2.

Knock-knock.

Who's there?

answer: _____

question: _____ who?

punch line: _____

3.

Knock-knock.

Who's there?

answer: _____

question: _____ *who?*

punch line: _____

4.

Knock-knock.

Who's there?

answer: _____

question: _____ *who?*

punch line: _____

5.

Knock-knock.

Who's there?

answer: _____

question: _____ *who?*

punch line: _____

A poem about a story:

_____

_____

_____

_____

_____

_____

_____

_____

_____

_____

_____

_____

_____

_____

A story about a poem:

Road Map of
MY
NEIGHBORHOOD
Showing
Possible Faerie
Paths

Sketches of phookas.

1. Animal form:

2. *Human form:*

SPRITE

Their wings resembled leaves,
but their faces seemed almost human.

FROM BOOK 2: THE SEEING STONE

SPRITES

I grew up in the city, but we would visit my
grandparents in the country for the holidays.
I hated it. You would think that it would be easy
to sleep with only the noises of crickets out
the window, but it's actually pretty impossible if
you're not used to it. My ears would strain for
the familiar sounds of cars and people and when
they didn't hear anything, they would strain even
harder. They would strain so hard that they
would wake me up so I could concentrate on
listening too.

And when I did hear something, it was hard
to figure out what it was. Branches from the
overgrown trees scratching against the aluminum
siding of the house sounded a lot like the claws of
a monster. A dog howling in the distance sounded
like how I figured a werewolf might sound. Dogs
sure didn't howl like that in the city.

But the worst thing of all was the darkness.
In the city, there were always lights

twinkling in the distance, neon signs brightening the streets underneath my window. Out in the country, at night, the sky was as black as the inside of a closet. Mom said my eyes would adjust, but they never did.

One weekend after Thanksgiving, I was lying in the bed in the guest room, next to Grandma's sewing machine and teetering stacks of fabric taller than me. I had the blanket pulled over my head in case anything was looking though the window, but I could see a little bit through a small hole in the fabric. More than anything, I wanted to put on the overhead light, but I knew some adult would come along and shut it off.

I tossed and turned, but when I closed my eyes, the darkness of my lids was too dark. The silence left me waiting for *something*. I didn't know what, but my heart raced regardless.

Opening my eyes, I saw lights outside the window, dozens of them, like strings of holiday twinklers. My bare feet hit the cold wooden floorboards before I could think about it. My fear was gone, replaced by a nameless excitement. My breath frosted the window glass as I stared out at the little creatures. They were tiny and winged, but they looked more like tiny people than bugs. They darted around a knot on the old oak tree that seemed to have swung open on tiny hinges. Looking closer, I saw some of them enter the tree. It was hollow, lit from the inside by their tiny, glowing bodies. I watched them out there, whirling through the air, for many minutes without them seeming to notice me, or me caring if they did.

Finally, cold and sleepy, I crept back to bed. As my eyes closed, my blurred vision seemed to turn the bright, flitting creatures into city lights. With that familiar sight in mind, I slipped off into sleep.

I don't know what those things were, but I haven't had any trouble sleeping out in the country since I saw them.

—Juan G.

ANALYSIS: Sprites sometimes take up residence in trees. This appears to be a rare sighting of these tiny faeries.
—H. B. & T. D.

Sometimes at night, I hear this creature:

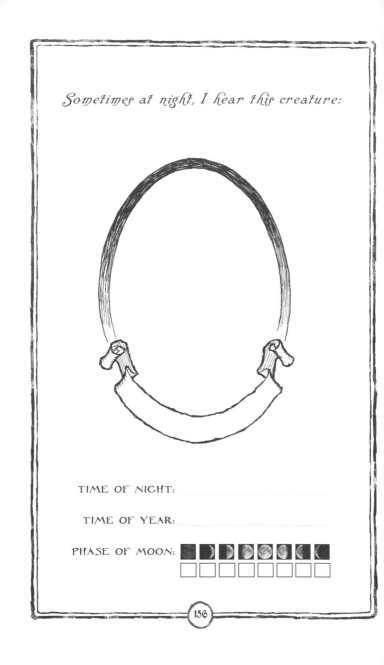

TIME OF NIGHT: _____

TIME OF YEAR: _____

PHASE OF MOON:

Here's what else I know about it:

_____

_____

_____

_____

_____

_____

_____

_____

_____

_____

_____

_____

_____

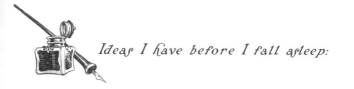

Ideas I have before I fall asleep:

1.

2.

3.

4.

5.

6.

7.

8.

9.

10.

11.

12.

13.

A dream I have over and over:

Commonly known as faeries, sprites look like a mix of humans, insects, and plants. A poem about a sprite that lives in the country:

_____

_____

_____

_____

_____

_____

_____

_____

_____

_____

_____

A poem about a sprite that lives in the city:

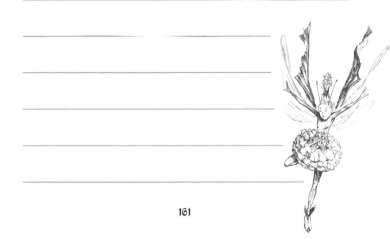

The view from my window:

The view from my window with a seeing stone:

This is what I would look like if I were a sprite:

This would be my sprite family:

STRAY SOD

He recalled something about people losing their way, even really close to home. . . .

FROM BOOK 3: LUCINDA'S SECRET

STRAY SOD

When I was about twelve, I stayed at my friend Rob's place longer than I should have. We'd been reading comics and making up new superheroes, like Monkey Man and Booger Boy, until we laughed so hard that chocolate milk shot out my nose and made me choke. When I looked at my watch, I realized I'd completely lost track of time and was going to be way late for dinner no matter what I did, but I thought that maybe there was a way I could avoid getting seriously punished.

There was this farm between Rob's house and my house and it was supposed to be haunted. My grandma told me that back in her day the family was pretty prosperous, but during the Depression the people who lived there wouldn't share any of their food, even with kids who came begging. A couple of years later, the whole family got sick and died, one right after another. For a while, after that, there was a guy who tried to keep horses on the farm, but they always got spooked, jumped over the fence, and galloped all around my backyard and the neighborhood. Seriously. I used to sink my hands in the prints their hooves made in the mud. But, by the time I was coming home from Rob's, no one lived on the farm.

I figured that our parents told us the property was haunted to keep us from playing there, because it was overgrown and split by a fast-moving river. Even though the place creeped me out and I usually avoided it, my plan was to cut through and run all the way home. If it worked, I would be late enough to get a lecture, but not so late that I'd get grounded.

I climbed over the old post fence and took off across the field. Long weeds and maple seedlings whipped against my jeans. A wind blew through the patches of trees, making them rustle in a way that sounded like eerie laughter. I ran faster.

Here's the weird thing about running—it

makes you feel like you're being chased. The faster I ran, the more I felt like there was something on my heels. I glanced back automatically and at the same moment, my foot dropped into a groundhog burrow. I went down hard on the dirt, twisting my ankle, skinning my hands, and knocking the breath out of my body.

Getting up slowly, I felt pretty stupid. There was nothing following me, nothing to be scared of except shadows. But as I looked around, I wasn't really sure if I'd been running in the right direction. I could hear the river and I could see clumps of trees, but none of it looked familiar. I started walking the way I thought was toward my house, but the closer I got, the more convinced I was that I still wasn't going the right way. Panic rose in me, making my heart beat as fast as if I were still running. My raw hands burned where I'd fallen on them. I turned around, walked a little ways, changed direction, and then changed direction again.

Then, across the field, I saw a light. Relief flooded me. It had to be the street lamp that was at the end of my street. I started toward it, not running because of my stiffening ankle, but walking pretty fast. I didn't care about getting in trouble anymore or about the fact I was late. I just wanted to get home.

I stepped into a more heavily wooded area. The thick ceiling of leaves made it harder to see, but I kept my eyes on the single, unwavering light. It was brighter now, closer, and I figured that the trees were what had kept me from seeing familiar landmarks. As soon as I got on the other side of them, I'd be home.

I started to speed up, even though I couldn't see really well. I was so happy to be that close.

A voice called my name. I stopped and heard it again. It sounded just like my mother's voice, but close by, as though she were standing right behind me. I whirled and saw nothing, but that pause made me stop and think. The light was really bright and yet

I didn't see any of the lights of any of the neighborhood windows or porches, which should have been visible if I really were that close.

I stopped and sat down, forcing myself to be calm. After a few moments of me just sitting there, I thought I felt the grass shift under my feet. That completely freaked me out. I was so scared that I didn't move until the sun came up.

That was when I realized I'd spent the night at the edge of the river. One more step and I would have slipped down the steep bank and fallen into the dark water that rushed by.

—Tom R.

ANALYSIS: Stray sod shifts under the feet of travelers, causing them to go astray even in familiar surroundings.
—H. B. & T. D.

This small creature enjoys playing tricks on people:

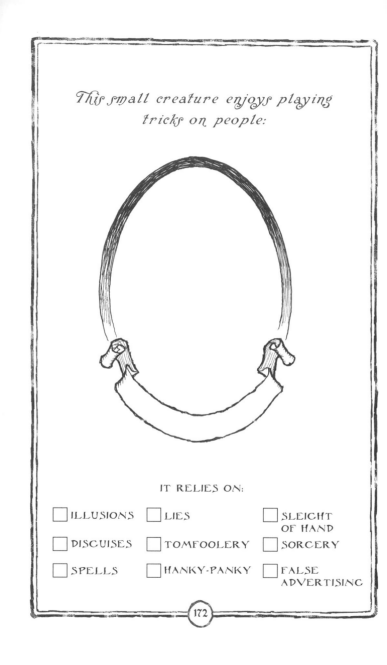

IT RELIES ON:

☐ ILLUSIONS ☐ LIES ☐ SLEIGHT OF HAND

☐ DISGUISES ☐ TOMFOOLERY ☐ SORCERY

☐ SPELLS ☐ HANKY-PANKY ☐ FALSE ADVERTISING

Here's what else I know about it:

_____

_____

_____

_____

_____

_____

_____

_____

_____

_____

_____

_____

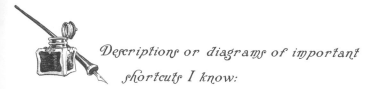

Descriptions or diagrams of important shortcuts I know:

1. *In my home:*

2. *In my neighborhood:*

❸ *In my school:*

❹ *Other:*

Map of
PLACES TO
WATCH FOR
STRAY SOD
(or Places Where
I Always Get Lost)

Pictures of my three favorite superheroes.

1.

Name:

Secret identity:

Super powers:

Name:

Secret identity:

Super powers:

2.

3.

Name:

Secret identity:

Super powers:

Three faerie superheroes I've made up:

Name:

Secret identity:

Super powers:

1.

2.

Name:

Secret identity:

Super powers:

Name:

Secret identity:

Super powers:

3.

My all-star baseball team of faerie creatures:

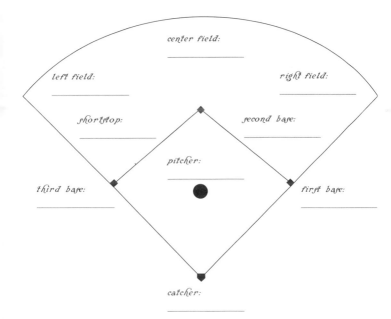

center field:
_____

left field:
_____

right field:
_____

shortstop:
_____

second base:
_____

pitcher:
_____

third base:
_____

first base:
_____

catcher:
_____

manager:
_____

pitching coach:
_____

hitting coach:
_____

Team batting order and other stats:

player:	field position:	bats right or left:	slugger (yes or no):	threat to steal (yes or no):
1.				
2.				
3.				
4.				
5.				
6.				
7.				
8.				
9.				

TROLL

The Guide had said that trolls weren't very smart.

FROM BOOK 2: THE SEEING STONE

TROLLS

One winter there was a terrible storm.
My dad got stuck sleeping in his office
in New York because all the trains were
snowed into place. When he called, he
told me that the whole city had come
to a standstill. Cars were buried so
deep that they looked like white hills
and the plows were barely making a
dent. The only people out on the street
were wading through the cold powder
on foot.

My mother got snowed in one town
over, at her sister's house. They'd
been out shopping or something and
had managed to get back to Aunt
Alicia's place before the snow hit. She
called me like a million times, talking
me through making a frozen pizza and
heating up some chicken noodle soup,
asking me if I needed her to try to
make it home. I told her I'd be fine.

I ate my pizza and soup in front

of the television and watched cartoons until I was too sleepy to keep my eyes open. But then, as I dragged myself off to my bedroom, I got kind of freaked out. I was in our ranch house all alone. In bed, I could hear sleet rattle off the roof and I could see jagged icicles hanging off the gutters outside my window.

When the cat jumped up on my bed, I yelped. I normally think of our tortoiseshell cat as annoying. She's old, and when she meows, it always sounds like someone just stepped on her tail. But right then, even though she scared me, I was glad to have something with me I petted her and she scooted up next to my body. Pretty soon I was asleep.

At first, when I woke up, I wasn't sure why I'd woken. It seemed colder than before and there was a tinkling sound outside my window as the wind knocked the icicles off the gutter. But there was another sound too, like someone was messing with one of the windows.

I leaped out of bed–almost falling on the floor–and listened for the sound. It came from my parents' room. I walked in and saw a monster through the lacy curtains.

It had a long nose, as pointed and twisting as one of the icicles, set on a huge, green face. Tiny, beady eyes were barely visible beneath shaggy, dark green brows. Long, branch-like fingers scraped at the window, then pushed it up. Cold air blew into the room, and the cat–who'd been following me–skittered under the bed.

I flicked on the lights. The creature shuffled back from the window, but didn't disappear. I could still see it out there, watching me through the curtains, gnashing its teeth.

"What are you?" I yelled. Despite my best intentions, my voice quavered.

"Troll," it said.

I didn't know anything about trolls. Nothing at all.

"The light will burn out," the troll said in a voice that was full of whispers. "And then I will come in."

"I'll turn on another light," I said.

"In a storm like this, your light could die. Anything could happen." That soft, persuasive voice made me shudder. It was right, but I didn't say so. I didn't say anything.

"Let's play a game while we wait," it said. "I will tell you a riddle and then you tell me one."

"What happens if I don't get one right?" I asked.

"Maybe I'll find the way to stop all the light."

I squeaked with terror. Could it really cut the power to the house? "What happens if you don't get one right?"

"Maybe I'll find another house with a child that is not so clever."

"Okay," I said. What else could I say? "I'll start."

The troll nodded and I racked my brain for ideas. We used to play riddle games in school, but I only remembered some of them.

"What has eyes but can't see?" I asked. It seemed kind of easy, but it was the only one I could think of.

The troll made a hissing laugh, like steam in a pot. "A potato. Now answer me this: The more you take away from me, the larger I get. What am I?"

I swallowed hard. My brain felt foggy with fear. I had to calm down and think this through. If something gets bigger when you take things away from it, then it must be a negative thing. A thing like nothing. A black hole. A hole! "A hole," I said, slumping onto my parents' bed with relief, sure that I had gotten it right.

The troll grunted. "Tell your riddle now."

Oh, right. I straightened up. "What kind of nut has no shell?" I actually thought that this one might have a chance. It wasn't the hardest riddle in the world, but it did assume a certain degree of knowledge about food that I wasn't sure the troll had.

It scowled and grumbled, and for a moment, I thought I had him. But then the troll grinned toothily. "Doughnut," it whispered. "Now it is my turn. Here is my riddle: What drapes us all in white and bites without teeth?"

I shivered in the breeze from the open window and knew I had the answer. "Frost," I said.

We went back and forth like that, answering and asking riddles all through the night. As dawn reddened the horizon, the troll asked me, "What can't you keep until you give?"

For the first time, I had no idea. I thought it must be something that wasn't tangible, something like love or hope, but I couldn't think of what.

I tried to think, but as time wore on, I knew I had no idea what the answer was supposed to be.

"Do you give up?" the troll asked, leaning close.

"No," I said quickly. "I'll get it."

The troll leaned forward, eagerness writ on its features. Long fingers snaked toward the open window, caressing the sill. "Now. Tell me the answer now or I win."

"The answer is . . . ," I said, stalling for seconds.

Just then, the first edge of the sun was visible in the distance. Light touched the troll and its skin went gray and hard. Fingers still reaching for me, it turned to stone. No longer did it look like a troll. Now it just seemed like a huge boulder that happened to be on our well-manicured lawn.

Just then, I found the answer that had eluded me. "A promise," I said aloud.

—Judy R.

ANALYSIS: Trolls are thought to turn to stone in sunlight. It is said that some boulders that seem to have faces in them were once trolls. —H. B. & T. D.

This creature only comes out at night:

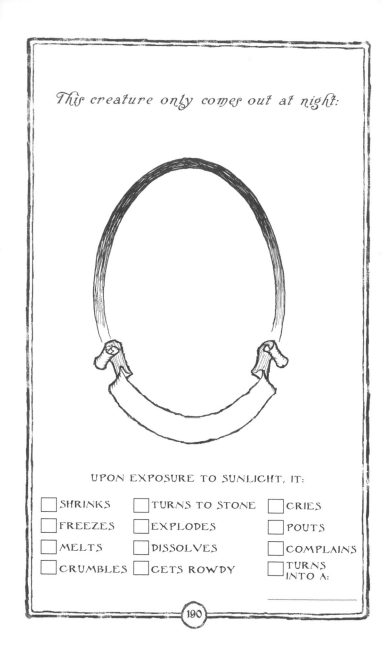

UPON EXPOSURE TO SUNLIGHT, IT:

☐ SHRINKS   ☐ TURNS TO STONE   ☐ CRIES

☐ FREEZES   ☐ EXPLODES   ☐ POUTS

☐ MELTS   ☐ DISSOLVES   ☐ COMPLAINS

☐ CRUMBLES ☐ GETS ROWDY   ☐ TURNS
                                 INTO A:

_____

Here's what else I know about it:

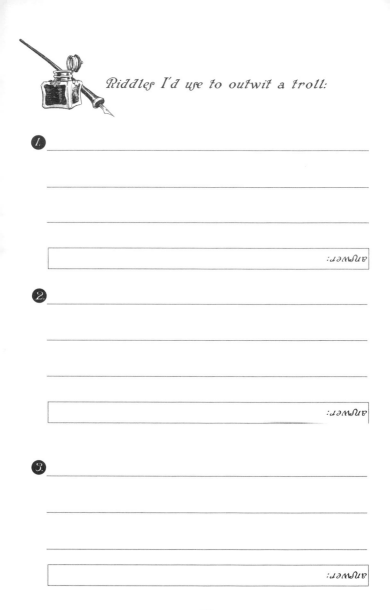

Riddles I'd use to outwit a troll:

1.

answer:

2.

answer:

3.

answer:

192

4. _____

_____

_____

answer:

5. _____

_____

_____

answer:

6. _____

_____

_____

answer:

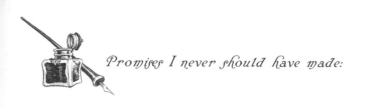

Promises I never should have made:

_____

_____

_____

_____

_____

_____

_____

_____

_____

_____

_____

_____

_____

Promises I'll keep forever:

Map of
MY
NEIGHBORHOOD
Showing Places
Where Trolls
Might Live

Diagram for a board game called
"TRICK THE TROLL"
in which players ask riddles and move
their pieces with each correct answer:

Design the game board:

Pictures or list of game pieces required to play:

Rules and instructions:

UNICORN

The horn that jutted from its forehead was twisted to an end that looked sharp.

FROM BOOK 3: LUCINDA'S SECRET

UNICORNS

My little sister has a ton of unicorns. She has stuffed animals, porcelain figurines, little plastic toys in pink and blue and yellow. They have the bodies and hooves of horses. Some of them have gold horns, but most of the horns are long and white, like the spiral of a shell. And, of course, they curl up in girls' laps like kittens.

They don't look anything like real unicorns.

Real unicorns are smaller than a horse and more slender. They look a little like deer, but they look a little like goats, too. Their toes are splayed and their horns look too big and heavy for their heads. But the most important difference is that they don't come in blue or pink or even really white. They're a muddy cream color, the way white socks get after you wear them a couple of times.

You're probably wondering how I know what unicorns look like, especially since I'm a boy, especially since I live in the city. Well, I'll tell you. I saw one at the zoo.

We had a school trip there. We were supposed to stick together and go see some boring exhibits, but there was this plan for what to do if you were lost. The teachers told us that if we got separated from the group, we were supposed to meet at the gates at two o'clock.

I figured I could go off, see all the stuff I wanted to see, then pretend it was unintentional.

At first it was great. I saw the pink-toed tarantulas that live together in groups, and I tapped the glass to make the hissing cockroach hiss at me. I even saw a bat that looks like a Chihuahua. But after a while I got lonely and thought that maybe I could catch up to the group. None of those things were as much fun by myself.

I passed the lions lounging on the pretend Serengeti, and the cheetahs. I came to the petting zoo. There were llamas and chinchillas and whatnot, but in with the goats was a weird animal that I'd never seen before. It was pale and looked a little like a deer.

I turned to a janitor sitting on a bench near a garbage can he'd just emptied and smoking a cigarette. He was an old guy with a face heavily lined with wrinkles, like dry earth that has started to crack.

"What's that?" I asked him, pointing to the animal.

"A unicorn," he said. I expected him to smile, but he looked as solemn and bored as he had a moment ago.

"It is not," I said. I hated it when adults tried to mess with my head.

He shrugged.

"If it's a unicorn, then where's its horn?" I demanded.

"Take a look for yourself." He stood up and put out his cigarette with his heel. Picking up the butt, he stuck it in the mound of garbage already on his cart and started to wheel it away.

I leaned out my hand to the deer-goat thing. It nuzzled my palm and as it did, I saw that at the center of its forehead there was a rough circle of cut bone, as though someone had hacked a long and majestic horn from its brow.

—Alex L.

ANALYSIS: This encounter is evidence that unicorns can live on without their horns, although it is unclear what magical properties they might still possess. —H. B. & T. D.

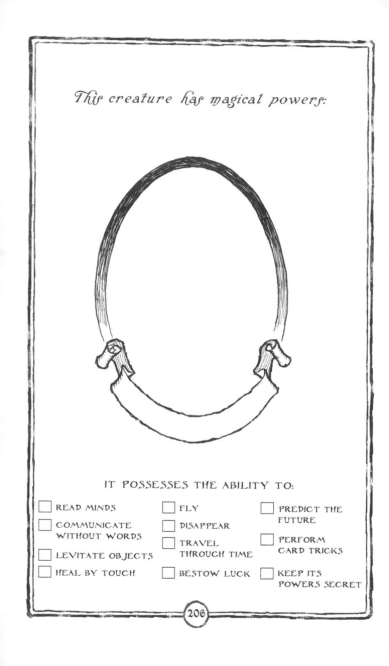

This creature has magical powers:

IT POSSESSES THE ABILITY TO:

- [ ] READ MINDS
- [ ] COMMUNICATE WITHOUT WORDS
- [ ] LEVITATE OBJECTS
- [ ] HEAL BY TOUCH
- [ ] FLY
- [ ] DISAPPEAR
- [ ] TRAVEL THROUGH TIME
- [ ] BESTOW LUCK
- [ ] PREDICT THE FUTURE
- [ ] PERFORM CARD TRICKS
- [ ] KEEP ITS POWERS SECRET

Here's what else I know about it:

_____

_____

_____

_____

_____

_____

_____

_____

_____

_____

_____

 *List of magical powers I'd like to have:*

1. *Physical powers:*

1.

2.

3.

4.

5.

6.

2. *Mental powers:*

1.

2.

3.

4.

5.

6.

3. Psychic powers:

1. _____

2. _____

3. _____

4. _____

5. _____

6. _____

4. Other really cool things I could do:

1. _____

2. _____

3. _____

4. _____

5. _____

6. _____

"THE MOST MAGICAL CREATURE OF ALL"

is the title of each of the following:

a *haiku:*

_____

_____

_____

a *poem:*

_____

_____

_____

_____

_____

_____

_____

a song:

A Chart of Observations of Fantastical Creatures

Fill in spaces with: **Y** = yes **N** = no **S** = sometimes
? = unknown **!** = oh yeah, in a big way

	FRIENDLY	FRIGHTENING	CUDDLY	GROTESQUE	CUTE	CARNIVOROUS	VEGETARIAN	SWEET TOOTH	SHAPE-SHIFTER	INTELLIGENT	NOCTURNAL	DIURNAL	MISCHIEVOUS	TRUSTWORTHY
Brownies														
Dragons														
Dwarves														
Elves														
Goblins														
Griffins														
Hobgoblins														
Knockers														
Ogres														
Phookas														
Sprites														
Stray Sod														
Trolls														
Unicorn														

A Chart of Observations of My Own Fantastical Creatures

NAME OF CREATURE	FRIENDLY	FRIGHTENING	CUDDLY	GROTESQUE	CUTE	CARNIVOROUS	VEGETARIAN	SWEET TOOTH	SHAPE-SHIFTER	INTELLIGENT	NOCTURNAL	DIURNAL	MISCHIEVOUS	TRUSTWORTHY

My Map of
the WORLD of
Fantastical
Creatures
Showing Many of
the Creatures Featured
in This Notebook

MORE
FANTASTICAL
OBSERVATIONS